Poetry

— for —

Little Ones

Volume 1

For my father, Tom Berrigan,
who gave me a love of poetry from the start.

For Virginia and Roxanne, you are my favorite poems.

For Nick, who lives the poetry with me.

Poetry for Little Ones

13-Digit ISBN: 978-1-64643-164-9
10-Digit ISBN: 1-64643-164-2

This book may be ordered by mail from the publisher. Please include $5.99 for postage and
handling. Please support your local bookseller first!

Books published by Cider Mill Press Book Publishers are available at special
discounts for bulk purchases in the United States by corporations, institutions, and
other organizations. For more information, please contact the publisher.

Cider Mill Press Book Publishers
"Where good books are ready for press"
501 Nelson Place
Nashville, Tennessee 37214

cidermillpress.com

Typography: ITC Caslon 224, Latienne Pro, VVDS Organum

Image Credits: Illustrations by Gail Yerrill

All vectors used under official license from Shutterstock.com.

Printed in Malaysia
23 24 25 26 27 COS 6 5 4 3 2

A Little Book of
Rhymes and Lullabies

Poetry
— for —
Little Ones

Compiled by
Delia Berrigan

Volume 1

CIDER MILL
PRESS

BOOK
PUBLISHERS

Introduction

My father raised me on Oscar Williams's *Immortal Poems of the English Language*. I was served up Housman, Keats, Shelley, Dickinson, and Whitman alongside Mother Goose and Shakespeare. Beyond the classic children's books that I was read and have in turn read to my own children, poetry opened my mind and my heart to a world of endless imagination and self-expression.

Great poems can be found for nearly every occasion.

I was adamant about passing down my love of reading to my children. Always one to follow the rules, I took seriously the guidelines from the American Academy of Pediatrics, who declare that it is never too early or too late to start reading to your children!

Pediatricians are promoting the five R's of early

education with young families:

- **Reading** together every day as a family activity;
- **Rhyming**, playing, talking, singing, and cuddling together throughout the day;
- Building **Routines** for meals, play, and sleep, which help children know what to expect and what is expected of them;
- Giving **Rewards** for everyday sucesses, understanding that praise from those closest to a child is a very potent reward; and
- Developing **Relationships** that are nurturing, purposeful, and lasting, which are the foundations of healthy early brain and child development.

Now, I may not necessarily embrace the old adage that an apple a day keeps the doctor away, but I do fully believe that reading *Poetry for Little Ones* daily brings you and your child closer together. As I set out to compile poetry, I gave myself some criteria:

1. It doesn't all have to be childlike or child-friendly. One of the first poems I ever memorized was "When I Was One-and-Twenty," by A. E. Housman. Did I know what it was about? Of

course not. How could a five-year-old understand a poem reminiscing about being a twenty-one-year-old? But was it fun to learn and repeat the rhyme? You bet! My brain enjoyed the rhyme and the vocabulary that I would otherwise not learn or hear without taking classes later in life.

2. Try to stay in the public domain, but go broader than the English canon. I like the public domain because you're more likely to find a poem that features on a print or postcard that you can purchase and put on display. But I also feel like it's important to expose folks to poetry beyond Shakespeare (not that I don't love Shakespeare—you'll see him frequently). It's tricky to find diverse and inclusive poems that are in the public domain. Those poems in the public domain are primarily much older and don't necessarily have the same cultural sensibilities as today. In the cases of those poems that probably wouldn't be written today, I think it's important to have a discussion about why and how something was viewed in the past versus how we see things with a bit more clarity and compassion in the present day.

3. Have fun! I've had such a lovely time reading

through books and pages of poems each day. I wish I had a book like *Poetry for Little Ones* to begin reading with my daughters from the very beginning, but I've been lucky enough to share the discoveries I've made—along with some old favorites—as I've put this together.

I hope you enjoy this book as much as I have enjoyed working on it. Poems are how we celebrate the joy, beauty, pain, and meaning of life. Celebrate a little every day.

If I Can Stop One Heart from Breaking

by Emily Dickinson

If I can stop one heart from breaking,
I shall not live in vain;
If I can ease one life the aching,
Or cool one pain,
Or help one fainting robin
Unto his nest again,
I shall not live in vain.

How Many Days
by Mother Goose

How many days has my baby to play?
Saturday, Sunday, Monday,
Tuesday, Wednesday, Thursday, Friday,
Saturday, Sunday, Monday.

Sonnet XV

by William Shakespeare

When I consider every thing that grows
Holds in perfection but a little moment,
That this huge stage presenteth nought but shows
Whereon the stars in secret influence comment;
When I perceive that men as plants increase,
Cheered and checked even by the selfsame sky,
Vaunt in their youthful sap, at height decrease,
And wear their brave state out of memory;
Then the conceit of this inconstant stay
Sets you most rich in youth before my sight,
Where wasteful Time debateth with decay
To change your day of youth to sullied night;
 And all in war with Time for love of you,
 As he takes from you, I engraft you new.

There Was an Old Woman Lived Under the Hill

by Mother Goose

There was an old woman lived under the hill,

And if she's not gone she lives there still.

Baked apples she sold, and cranberry pies,

And she's the old woman that never told lies.

April Flowers

by Pauline Jenks

Where forest tangle is the wildest
    And all is wet with April showers,
And where the wind's fierce roar is mildest,
    'Tis there you find the spring's first flowers.
Where thrush sings on the leafless tree,
    Where all is lonely, still, and wet,
You'll see a fair anemone,
    And possibly a violet.

Morning Song of the Bees

by Louisa May Alcott

"Awake! awake! for the earliest gleam
Of golden sunlight shines
On the rippling waves, that brightly flow
Beneath the flowering vines.
Awake! awake! for the low, sweet chant
Of the wild-birds' morning hymn
Comes floating by on the fragrant air,
Through the forest cool and dim;
Then spread each wing,
And work, and sing,
Through the long, bright sunny hours;
O'er the pleasant earth
We journey forth,
For a day among the flowers.

"Awake! awake! for the summer wind
Hath bidden the blossoms unclose,

Hath opened the violet's soft blue eye,
And wakened the sleeping rose.
And lightly they wave on their slender stems
Fragrant, and fresh, and fair,
Waiting for us, as we singing come
To gather our honey-dew there.
Then spread each wing,
And work, and sing,
Through the long, bright sunny hours;
O'er the pleasant earth
We journey forth,
For a day among the flowers!"

Invitation to the Ant

by Caroline Howard Gilman

Come here, little ant,
For the pretty bird can't.
I want you to come,
And live at my home;

I know you will stay,
And help me to play.
Stop making that hill,
Little ant, and be still.

Come, creep to my feet,
Here is sugar to eat.
Say, are you not weary,
My poor little deary,

With bearing that load,
Across the wide road?

Leave your hill now, to me,
And then you shall see,

That by filling my hand,
I can pile up the sand,
And save you the pains,
Of bringing these grains.

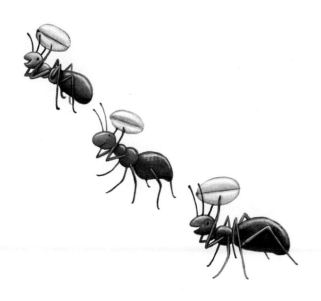

Pat a Cake, Pat a Cake

by Mother Goose

Pat a cake, pat a cake,

Baker's man!

So I do, master, as fast as I can.

Pat it, and prick it,

And mark it with T.

And then it will serve

For Tommy and me.

Sonnet XVIII

by William Shakespeare

Shall I compare thee to a summer's day?
Thou art more lovely and more temperate:
Rough winds do shake the darling buds of May,
And summer's lease hath all too short a date;
Sometime too hot the eye of heaven shines,
And often is his gold complexion dimm'd,
And every fair from fair sometime declines,
By chance, or nature's changing course untrimm'd:
But thy eternal summer shall not fade,
Nor lose possession of that fair thou ow'st,
Nor shall death brag thou wander'st in his shade,
When in eternal lines to time thou grow'st,
    So long as men can breathe, or eyes can see,
    So long lives this, and this gives life to thee.

I'm Nobody!
Who Are You?

by Emily Dickinson

I'm nobody! Who are you?

Are you nobody, too?

Then there's a pair of us—don't tell!

They'd banish us, you know.

How dreary to be somebody!

How public, like a frog

To tell your name the livelong day

To an admiring bog!

A Boy Scouts' Patrol Song

by Rudyard Kipling

These are *our* regulations,

There's just one law for the Scout

And the first and the last, and the present and
the past,

And the future and the perfect is "Look out!"

I, thou and he, look out!

We, ye and they, look out!

Though you didn't or you wouldn't

Or you hadn't or you couldn't;

You jolly well *must* look out!

Look out, when you start for the day

That your kit is packed to your mind;

There is no use going away

With half of it left behind.

Look out that your laces are tight,

And your boots are easy and stout,

Or you'll end with a blister at night.

(Chorus) All Patrols look out!

Look out for the birds of the air,
Look out for the beasts of the field—
They'll tell you how and where
The other side's concealed.
When the blackbird bolts from the copse,
Or the cattle are staring about,
The wise commander stops
And *(chorus)* All Patrols look out!

Look out when your front is clear,
And you feel you are bound to win.
Look out for your flank and your rear—
That's where surprises begin.
For the rustle that isn't a rat,
For the splash that isn't a trout,
For the boulder that may be a hat
(Chorus) All Patrols look out!

For the innocent knee-high grass,
For the ditch that never tells,
Look out! Look out ere you pass—
And look out for everything else!
A sign mis-read as you run
May turn retreat to a rout—
For all things under the sun
(Chorus) All Patrols look out!

Look out when your temper goes
At the end of a losing game;
When your boots are too tight for your toes;
And you answer and argue and blame.
It's the hardest part of the Law,
But it has to be learnt by the Scout—
For whining and shirking and "jaw"
(Chorus) All Patrols look out!

Katy-Did–Katy-Didn't
by Mary Eleanor Wilkins Freeman

Who was Katy, who was she,
  That you prate of her so long?
Was she just a little lassie
  Full of smiles and wiles and song?

Did she spill the cups o' dew
  Filled for helpless, thirsty posies?
Did she tie a butterfly
  Just beyond the reach o' roses?

Slandered she some sweet dumb thing?
  Called a tulip dull and plain,
Said the clover had no fragrance,
  And the lily had a stain?

Did she mock the pansies' faces,
  Or a grandpa-longlegs flout?

Did she chase the frightened fireflies
  Till their pretty lamps went out?

Well, whatever 'twas, O Katy!
  We believe no harm of you;
And we'll join your stanch defenders,
  Singing "Katy-didn't," too.

Boys and Girls, Come Out to Play

by Mother Goose

Boys and girls, come out to play,
The moon does shine as bright as day,
Leave your supper, and leave your sleep,
And meet your playfellows in the street;
Come with a whoop, and come with a call,
And come with a good will, or not at all.
Up the ladder and down the wall,
A halfpenny roll will serve us all.
You find milk and I'll find flour,
And we'll have pudding in half an hour.

Sonnet LXXV

by William Shakespeare

So are you to my thoughts as food to life,
Or as sweet-season'd showers are to the ground;
And for the peace of you I hold such strife
As 'twixt a miser and his wealth is found.
Now proud as an enjoyer, and anon
Doubting the filching age will steal his treasure;
Now counting best to be with you alone,
Then better'd that the world may see my pleasure:
Sometime all full with feasting on your sight,
And by and by clean starved for a look;
Possessing or pursuing no delight,
Save what is had, or must from you be took.
    Thus do I pine and surfeit day by day,
    Or gluttoning on all, or all away.

Humpty Dumpty

by Mother Goose

Humpty Dumpty sat on a wall, Humpty Dumpty
  had a great fall;

All the King's horses and all the King's men

Couldn't put Humpty Dumpty together again.

The Star

by Sara Teasdale

A white star born in the evening glow
Looked to the round green world below,
And saw a pool in a wooded place
That held like a jewel her mirrored face.
She said to the pool: "Oh, wondrous deep,
I love you, I give you my light to keep.
Oh, more profound than the moving sea
That never has shown myself to me!
Oh, fathomless as the sky is far,
Hold forever your tremulous star!"
But out of the woods as night grew cool
A brown pig came to the little pool;
It grunted and splashed and waded in
And the deepest place but reached its chin.
The water gurgled with tender glee
And the mud churned up in it turbidly.
The star grew pale and hid her face
In a bit of floating cloud like lace.

The Butterfly's Day

by Emily Dickinson

From cocoon forth a butterfly
As lady from her door
Emerged—a summer afternoon—
Repairing everywhere,

Without design, that I could trace,
Except to stray abroad
On miscellaneous enterprise
The clovers understood.

Her pretty parasol was seen
Contracting in a field
Where men made hay, then struggling hard
With an opposing cloud,

Where parties, phantom as herself,
To Nowhere seemed to go

In purposeless circumference,
As 't were a tropic show.

And notwithstanding bee that worked,
And flower that zealous blew,
This audience of idleness
Disdained them, from the sky,

Till sundown crept, a steady tide,
And men that made the hay,
And afternoon, and butterfly,
Extinguished in its sea.

Looking for the Fairies

by Julia Bacon

I've peeped in many a bluebell,
And crept among the flowers,
And hunted in the acorn cups,
And in the woodland bowers;
And shook the yellow daffodils,
And searched the gardens round,
A-looking for the little folk
I never, never found.

I've lingered till the setting sun
Threw out a golden sheen,
In hope to see a fairy troop
Come dancing on the green;
And marveled that they did not come
To revel in the air,
And wondered if they slept, and where
Their hiding-places were.

I've wandered with a timid step
Beneath the moon's pale light,
And every blazing dewdrop seemed
To be a tiny sprite;
And listened with suspended breath,
Among the grand old trees,
For fairy music floating soft
Upon the evening breeze.

Ah me! those pleasant sunny days
In youthful fancies wild,—Rambling through the
wooded dells,
A careless, happy child!
And now I sit and sigh to think
Age from childhood varies,
And never more may we be found
Looking for the fairies.

Hickory, Dickory

by Mother Goose

Hickory, dickory, dock,
The mouse ran up the clock;
The clock struck one, and down he run,
Hickory, dickory, dock.

Sonnet V

by William Shakespeare

Those hours, that with gentle work did frame
The lovely gaze where every eye doth dwell,
Will play the tyrants to the very same
And that unfair which fairly doth excel;
For never-resting time leads summer on
To hideous winter, and confounds him there;
Sap checked with frost, and lusty leaves quite
    gone,
Beauty o'er-snowed and bareness every where:
Then were not summer's distillation left,
A liquid prisoner pent in walls of glass,
Beauty's effect with beauty were bereft,
Nor it, nor no remembrance what it was:
    But flowers distill'd, though they with winter
      meet,
    Leese but their show; their substance still lives
      sweet.

The Children's Hour

by Henry Wadsworth Longfellow

Between the dark and the daylight,
     When the night is beginning to lower,
Comes a pause in the day's occupations,
     That is known as the Children's Hour.

I hear in the chamber above me
     The patter of little feet,
The sound of a door that is opened,
     And voices soft and sweet.

From my study I see in the lamplight,
     Descending the broad hall stair,
Grave Alice, and laughing Allegra,
     And Edith with golden hair.

A whisper, and then a silence:
     Yet I know by their merry eyes

They are plotting and planning together
   To take me by surprise.

A sudden rush from the stairway,
   A sudden raid from the hall!
By three doors left unguarded
   They enter my castle wall!

They climb up into my turret
   O'er the arms and back of my chair;
If I try to escape, they surround me;
   They seem to be everywhere.

They almost devour me with kisses,
   Their arms about me entwine,
Till I think of the Bishop of Bingen
   In his Mouse-Tower on the Rhine!

Do you think, O blue-eyed banditti,
   Because you have scaled the wall,

Such an old mustache as I am
    Is not a match for you all!

I have you fast in my fortress,
    And will not let you depart,
But put you down into the dungeon
    In the round-tower of my heart.

And there will I keep you forever,
    Yes, forever and a day,
Till the walls shall crumble to ruin,
    And molder in dust away!

Wee Willie Winkie

by Mother Goose

Wee Willie Winkie runs through the town,
Upstairs and downstairs in his nightgown;
Tapping at the window, crying at the lock,
"Are the babes in their beds, for it's now ten
o'clock?"

When I Was One-and-Twenty

by A. E. Housman

When I was one-and-twenty
I heard a wise man say,
"Give crowns and pounds and guineas
But not your heart away;
Give pearls away and rubies
But keep your fancy free."
But I was one-and-twenty,
No use to talk to me.

When I was one-and-twenty
I heard him say again,
"The heart out of the bosom
Was never given in vain;
'Tis paid with sighs a plenty
And sold for endless rue."
And I am two-and-twenty,
And oh, 'tis true, 'tis true.

Bye, Baby Bunting

by Mother Goose

Bye, baby bunting,
Father's gone a hunting,
Mother's gone a milking,
Sister's gone a silking,
And brother's gone to buy a skin,
To wrap the baby bunting in.

The Bee Is Not Afraid of Me

by Emily Dickinson

The bee is not afraid of me,
I know the butterfly;
The pretty people in the woods
Receive me cordially.

The brooks laugh louder when I come,
The breezes madder play.
Wherefore, mine eyes, thy silver mists?
Wherefore, O summer's day?

Tree Feelings

by Charlotte Perkins Gilman

I wonder if they like it—being trees?

I suppose they do. It must feel good to have the
ground so flat,

And feel yourself stand right straight up like that—

So stiff in the middle—and then branch at ease,

Big boughs that arch, small ones that bend
and blow,

And all those fringy leaves that flutter so.

You'd think they'd break off at the lower end

When the wind fills them, and their great
heads bend.

But then you think of all the roots they drop,

As much at bottom as there is on top,—

A double tree, widespread in earth and air

Like a reflection in the water there.

I guess they like to stand still in the sun

And just breathe out and in, and feel the cool
sap run;

And like to feel the rain run through their hair
And slide down to the roots and settle there.
But I think they like wind best. From the light
  touch
That lets the leaves whisper and kiss so much,
To the great swinging, tossing, flying wide,
And all the time so stiff and strong inside!
And the big winds, that pull, and make them feel
How long their roots are, and the earth how leal!

And O the blossoms! And the wild seeds lost!
And jeweled martyrdom of fiery frost!
And fruit-trees. I'd forgotten. No cold gem,
But to be apples—And bow down with them!

As I Grew Older

by Langston Hughes

It was a long time ago.
I have almost forgotten my dream.
But it was there then,
In front of me,
Bright like a sun—
My dream.
And then the wall rose,
Rose slowly,
Slowly,
Between me and my dream.
Rose until it touched the sky—
The wall.
Shadow.
I am black.
I lie down in the shadow.
No longer the light of my dream before me,
Above me.

Only the thick wall.
Only the shadow.
My hands!
My dark hands!
Break through the wall!
Find my dream!
Help me to shatter this darkness,
To smash this night,
To break this shadow
Into a thousand lights of sun,
Into a thousand whirling dreams
Of sun!

Birches

by Robert Frost

When I see birches bend to left and right

Across the lines of straighter darker trees,

I like to think some boy's been swinging them.

But swinging doesn't bend them down to stay

As ice-storms do. Often you must have seen them

Loaded with ice a sunny winter morning

After a rain. They click upon themselves

As the breeze rises, and turn many-colored

As the stir cracks and crazes their enamel.

Soon the sun's warmth makes them shed crystal shells

Shattering and avalanching on the snow-crust—

Such heaps of broken glass to sweep away

You'd think the inner dome of heaven had fallen.

They are dragged to the withered bracken by the load,

And they seem not to break; though once they are bowed

So low for long, they never right themselves:
You may see their trunks arching in the woods
Years afterwards, trailing their leaves on the
ground
Like girls on hands and knees that throw their
hair
Before them over their heads to dry in the sun.
But I was going to say when Truth broke in
With all her matter-of-fact about the ice-storm
(Now am I free to be poetical?)
I should prefer to have some boy bend them
As he went out and in to fetch the cows—
Some boy too far from town to learn baseball,
Whose only play was what he found himself,
Summer or winter, and could play alone.
One by one he subdued his father's trees
By riding them down over and over again
Until he took the stiffness out of them,
And not one but hung limp, not one was left
For him to conquer. He learned all there was
To learn about not launching out too soon

And so not carrying the tree away

Clear to the ground. He always kept his poise

To the top branches, climbing carefully

With the same pains you use to fill a cup

Up to the brim, and even above the brim.

Then he flung outward, feet first, with a swish,

Kicking his way down through the air to the
     ground.

So was I once myself a swinger of birches.

And so I dream of going back to be.

It's when I'm weary of considerations,

And life is too much like a pathless wood

Where your face burns and tickles with the
     cobwebs

Broken across it, and one eye is weeping

From a twig's having lashed across it open.

I'd like to get away from earth awhile

And then come back to it and begin over.

May no fate willfully misunderstand me

And half grant what I wish and snatch me away

Not to return. Earth's the right place for love:

I don't know where it's likely to go better.
I'd like to go by climbing a birch tree,
And climb black branches up a snow-white trunk
Toward heaven, till the tree could bear no more,
But dipped its top and set me down again.
That would be good both going and coming back.
One could do worse than be a swinger of birches.

Sonnet VIII

by William Shakespeare

Music to hear, why hear'st thou music sadly?

Sweets with sweets war not, joy delights in joy:

Why lov'st thou that which thou receiv'st not
gladly,

Or else receiv'st with pleasure thine annoy?

If the true concord of well-tuned sounds,

By unions married, do offend thine ear,

They do but sweetly chide thee, who confounds

In singleness the parts that thou shouldst bear.

Mark how one string, sweet husband to another,

Strikes each in each by mutual ordering;

Resembling sire and child and happy mother,

Who, all in one, one pleasing note do sing:

> Whose speechless song being many, seeming
> one,

> Sings this to thee: "Thou single wilt prove
> none."

Sing a Song of Sixpence

by Mother Goose

Sing a song of sixpence, a bag full of rye,

Four and twenty blackbirds baked in a pie:

When the pie was opened, the birds began to
sing;

And wasn't this a dainty dish to set before the
king?

The king was in the parlor, counting out his
money;

The queen was in the kitchen, eating bread and
honey;

The maid was in the garden, hanging out the
clothes,

There came a little blackbird and nipt off her
nose.

The Grass

by Emily Dickinson

The grass so little has to do,—
A sphere of simple green,
With only butterflies to brood,
And bees to entertain,

And stir all day to pretty tunes
The breezes fetch along,
And hold the sunshine in its lap
And bow to everything;

And thread the dews all night, like pearls,
And make itself so fine,—
A duchess were too common
For such a noticing.

And even when it dies, to pass
In odors so divine,

As lowly spices gone to sleep,
Or amulets of pine.

And then to dwell in sovereign barns,
And dream the days away,—
The grass so little has to do,
I wish I were the hay!

My Shadow

by Robert Louis Stevenson

I have a little shadow that goes in and out with me,

And what can be the use of him is more than I can
see.

He is very, very like me from the heels up to the
head;

And I see him jump before me, when I jump into
my bed.

The funniest thing about him is the way he likes
to grow—

Not at all like proper children, which is always
very slow;

For he sometimes shoots up taller like an india-
rubber ball,

And he sometimes gets so little that there's none
of him at all.

He hasn't got a notion of how children ought to
play,

And can only make a fool of me in every sort of
way.

He stays so close beside me, he's a coward you
can see;

I'd think shame to stick to nursie as that shadow
sticks to me!

One morning, very early, before the sun was up,

I rose and found the shining dew on every
buttercup;

But my lazy little shadow, like an arrant sleepy-
head,

Had stayed at home behind me and was fast
asleep in bed.

The Cuckoo Is
a Bonny Bird

by Mother Goose

The Cuckoo is a bonny bird,
She sings as she flies,
She brings us good tidings,
And tells us no lies.
She sucks little bird's eggs
To make her voice clear,
And never cries Cuckoo!
Till Spring of the year.

Sonnet XCVIII

by William Shakespeare

From you have I been absent in the spring,
When proud-pied April, dress'd in all his trim,
Hath put a spirit of youth in every thing,
That heavy Saturn laugh'd and leap'd with him.
Yet nor the lays of birds, nor the sweet smell
Of different flowers in odor and in hue,
Could make me any summer's story tell,
Or from their proud lap pluck them where they
   grew:
Nor did I wonder at the lilies white,
Nor praise the deep vermilion in the rose;
They were but sweet, but figures of delight,
Drawn after you, you pattern of all those.
   Yet seem'd it winter still, and you away,
   As with your shadow I with these did play.

Laugh and Be Merry
by John Masefield

Laugh and be merry, remember, better the world
    with a song,

Better the world with a blow in the teeth of a
    wrong.

Laugh, for the time is brief, a thread the length
    of a span.

Laugh and be proud to belong to the old proud
    pageant of man.

Laugh and be merry: remember, in olden time.

God made Heaven and Earth for joy He took in a
    rhyme,

Made them, and filled them full with the strong
    red wine of

His mirth

The splendid joy of the stars: the joy of the earth.

So we must laugh and drink from the deep blue
    cup of the sky,

Join the jubilant song of the great stars sweeping
by,

Laugh, and battle, and work, and drink of the
wine outpoured

In the dear green earth, the sign of the joy of the
Lord.

Laugh and be merry together, like brothers akin,

Guesting awhile in the rooms of a beautiful inn,

Glad till the dancing stops, and the lilt of the
music ends.

Laugh till the game is played; and be you merry,
my friends.

As Children Bid the Guest Good-Night

by Emily Dickinson

As children bid the guest good-night,
And then reluctant turn,
My flowers raise their pretty lips,
Then put their nightgowns on.

As children caper when they wake,
Merry that it is morn,
My flowers from a hundred cribs
Will peep, and prance again.

In Frogland

by Gertrude Heath

Have you heard of the country of Bogland,
In the famous Kingdom of Frogland?
Where each plump mother frog
On a water-soaked log
Rocks Johnny and Peter and Polly Wog?

At night in this country of Bogland,
In this famous Kingdom of Frogland,
Have you heard the poor mother
Scold Pete and his brother,
And the froggies in turn all scolding each other?

In this curious country of Bogland,
In the famous Kingdom of Frogland,
Frogs are naughty, I fear,
Each night of the year;
Just listen some evening and you will hear!

The Little Seed

by Christina Moody

A little seed fell to the earth,
'Twas the seed of an apple tree.
'Twas too small to grow as I could plainly see—
Why it wasn't as large as a pea.

But the little seed planned of days to come,
When his body would be great and tall,
But how could that be, when he was so wee,
He could scarcely be seen at all?

By and by the seed broke in twain,
'Twas the death of him I said,
But instead of death, a pretty stem,
Lifted up his little green head.

The stem grew up with perfect grace
And looked with wondering eyes,

At the painting of Nature's wonderful art,
Until he became very wise.

Little leaflets too came forth,
With beauty that can't be told.
So the seed that was wee, grew into a tree
'Twas a wonderful sight to behold.

Sonnet CII

by William Shakespeare

My love is strengthen'd, though more weak in
   seeming;
I love not less, though less the show appear;
That love is merchandiz'd, whose rich
   esteeming,
The owner's tongue doth publish everywhere.
Our love was new, and then but in the spring,
When I was wont to greet it with my lays;
As Philomel in summer's front doth sing,
And stops her pipe in growth of riper days:
Not that the summer is less pleasant now
Than when her mournful hymns did hush the
   night,
But that wild music burdens every bough,
And sweets grown common lose their dear delight.
   Therefore like her, I sometime hold my tongue:
   Because I would not dull you with my song.

Hush-a-Bye, Baby

by Mother Goose

Hush-a-bye, baby, upon the tree top,

When the wind blows the cradle will rock;

When the bough breaks the cradle will fall,

Down tumble cradle and baby and all.

Summer Shower

by Emily Dickinson

A drop fell on the apple tree,
Another on the roof;
A half a dozen kissed the eaves,
And made the gables laugh.

A few went out to help the brook,
That went to help the sea.
Myself conjectured, Were they pearls,
What necklaces could be!

The dust replaced in hoisted roads,
The birds jocoser sung;
The sunshine threw his hat away,
The orchards spangles hung.

The breezes brought dejected lutes,
And bathed them in the glee;

The East put out a single flag,
And signed the fete away.

Lavender Blue,
and Rosemary Green
by Mother Goose

Lavender blue, and Rosemary green,
When I am king, you shall be queen,
Call up my maids at four of the clock,
Some to the wheel, and some to the rock,
Some to make hay, and some to shell corn,
And you and I shall keep the bed warm.

The Swing

by Robert Louis Stevenson

How do you like to go up in a swing,
  Up in the air so blue?
Oh, I do think it the pleasantest thing
  Ever a child can do!

Up in the air and over the wall,
  Till I can see so wide,
Rivers and trees and cattle and all
  Over the countryside—

Till I look down on the garden green,
  Down on the roof so brown—
Up in the air I go flying again,
  Up in the air and down!

The Wild Rabbits

by J. Steeple Davis

Among the sand-hills,
Near by the sea,
Wild young rabbits
Were seen by me.

They live in burrows
With winding ways,
And there they shelter
On rainy days.

The mother rabbits
Make cozy nests,
With hairy linings
From their breasts.

The tender young ones
Are nursed and fed,

And safely hidden
In this warm bed.

And when they are older,
They all come out
Upon the sand-hills,
And frisk about.

They play, and nibble
The long, dry grass,
But scamper away
Whenever you pass.

If

by Rudyard Kipling

If you can keep your head when all about you

Are losing theirs and blaming it on you;

If you can trust yourself when all men doubt
  you,

But make allowance for their doubting too;

If you can wait and not be tired by waiting,

Or being lied about, don't deal in lies,

Or being hated, don't give way to hating,

And yet don't look too good, nor talk too wise:

If you can dream, and not make dreams your
  master;

If you can think, and not make thoughts your
  aim;

If you can meet with Triumph and Disaster

And treat those two imposters just the same;

If you can bear to hear the truth you've spoken

Twisted by knaves to make a trap for fools,

Or watch the things you gave your life to, broken,
And stoop and build 'em up with worn-out tools;

If you can make one heap of all your winnings
And risk it on one turn of pitch-and-toss,
And lose, and start again at your beginnings
And never breathe a word about your loss;
If you can force your heart and nerve and sinew
To serve your turn long after they are gone,
And so hold on when there is nothing in you
Except the Will which says to them: "Hold on!"

If you can talk with crowds and keep your virtue,
Or walk with kings, nor lose the common touch,
If neither foes nor loving friends can hurt you,
If all men count with you, but none too much;
If you can fill the unforgiving minute
With sixty seconds' worth of distance run,
Yours is the Earth and everything that's in it,
And, which is more, you'll be a Man, my son!

A Needle's Eye

by W. B. Yeats

All the stream that's roaring by
Came out of a needle's eye;
Things unborn, things that are gone,
From needle's eye still goad it on.

A Night-Piece
by William Wordsworth

The sky is overcast

With a continuous cloud of texture close,

Heavy and wan, all whitened by the Moon,

Which through that veil is indistinctly seen,

A dull, contracted circle, yielding light

So feebly spread, that not a shadow falls,

Checkering the ground—from rock, plant, tree,
   or tower.

At length a pleasant instantaneous gleam

Startles the pensive traveller while he treads

His lonesome path, with unobserving eye

Bent earthwards; he looks up—the clouds are
   split

Asunder,—and above his head he sees

The clear Moon, and the glory of the heavens.

There, in a black-blue vault she sails along,

Followed by multitudes of stars, that, small

And sharp, and bright, along the dark abyss

Drive as she drives: how fast they wheel away,

Yet vanish not!—the wind is in the tree,

But they are silent;—still they roll along

Immeasurably distant; and the vault,

Built round by those white clouds, enormous
 clouds,

Still deepens its unfathomable depth.

At length the Vision closes; and the mind,

Not undisturbed by the delight it feels,

Which slowly settles into peaceful calm,

Is left to muse upon the solemn scene.

Heigh Ding a Ding

by Mother Goose

Heigh ding a ding, what shall I sing?

How many holes in a skimmer?

Four and twenty. I'm half starving!

Mother, pray give me some dinner.

Sonnet CXVI

by William Shakespeare

Let me not to the marriage of true minds
Admit impediments. Love is not love
Which alters when it alteration finds,
Or bends with the remover to remove:
O, no! it is an ever-fixed mark,
That looks on tempests and is never shaken;
It is the star to every wandering bark,
Whose worth's unknown, although his height
   be taken.
Love's not Time's fool, though rosy lips and
   cheeks
Within his bending sickle's compass come;
Love alters not with his brief hours and weeks,
But bears it out even to the edge of doom.
    If this be error and upon me prov'd,
    I never writ, nor no man ever lov'd.

We Play at Paste

by Emily Dickinson

We play at paste,
Till qualified for pearl,
Then drop the paste,
And deem ourself a fool.
The shapes, though, were similar,
And our new hands
Learned gem-tactics
Practicing sands.

A Fragment

by Henry Wadsworth Longfellow

Awake! arise! the hour is late!
　Angels are knocking at thy door!
They are in haste and cannot wait,
　And once departed come no more.

Awake! arise! the athlete's arm
　Loses its strength by too much rest;
The fallow land, the untilled farm
　Produces only weeds at best.

A Dream

by Edgar Allan Poe

In visions of the dark night
I have dreamed of joy departed
But a waking dream of life and light
Hath left me broken-hearted.

Ah! what is not a dream by day
To him whose eyes are cast
On things around him with a ray
Turned back upon the past?

That holy dream that holy dream,
While all the world were chiding,
Hath cheered me as a lovely beam,
A lonely spirit guiding.

What though that light, thro' storm and night,
So trembled from afar

What could there be more purely bright
In Truth's day star?

London Bridge

by Mother Goose

London bridge is broken down,
Dance over my Lady Lee,
London bridge is broken down,
With a gay ladye.
How shall we build it up again?
Dance over my Lady Lee,
How shall we build it up again?
With a gay ladye.
We'll build it up with gravel and stone,
Dance over my Lady Lee,
We'll build it up with gravel and stone,
With a gay ladye.
Gravel and stone will be washed away,
Dance over my Lady Lee,
Gravel and stone will be washed away,
With a gay ladye.
We'll build it up with iron and steel,

Dance over my Lady Lee,
We'll build it up with iron and steel,
With a gay ladye.
Iron and steel will bend and break,
Dance over my Lady Lee,
Iron and steel will bend and break,
With a gay ladye.
We'll build it up with silver and gold,
Dance over my Lady Lee,
We'll build it up with silver and gold,
With a gay ladye.
Silver and gold will be stolen away,
Dance over my Lady Lee,
Silver and gold will be stolen away,
With a gay ladye.
We'll set a man to watch it then,
Dance over my Lady Lee,
We'll set a man to watch it then,
With a gay ladye.
Suppose the man should fall asleep,

Dance over my Lady Lee,
Suppose the man should fall asleep,
With a gay ladye.
We'll put a pipe into his mouth,
Dance over my Lady Lee,
We'll put a pipe into his mouth,
With a gay ladye.

The Ostrich

by Mary Eleanor Wilkins Freeman

The ostrich is a silly bird,
With scarcely any mind.
He often runs so very fast,
He leaves himself behind.

And when he gets there, he has to stand
And hang about all night,
Without a blessed thing to do
Until he comes in sight.

Sonnet XI

by William Shakespeare

As fast as thou shalt wane, so fast thou grow'st,

In one of thine, from that which thou departest;

And that fresh blood which youngly thou
bestow'st,

Thou mayst call thine when thou from youth
convertest,

Herein lives wisdom, beauty, and increase;

Without this folly, age, and cold decay:

If all were minded so, the times should cease

And threescore year would make the world away.

Let those whom nature hath not made for store,

Harsh, featureless, and rude, barrenly perish:

Look, whom she best endow'd, she gave thee
more;

Which bounteous gift thou shouldst in bounty
cherish:

She carv'd thee for her seal, and meant thereby,

Thou shouldst print more, not let that copy die.

Rub-a-Dub

by Mother Goose

Hey rub-a-dub, ho rub-a-dub, three maids in
 a tub,
And who do you think was there?
The butcher, the baker, the candlestick-maker,
And all of them gone to the fair.

A Day

by Emily Dickinson

I'll tell you how the sun rose,—
A ribbon at a time.
The steeples swam in amethyst,
The news like squirrels ran.

The hills untied their bonnets,
The bobolinks begun.
Then I said softly to myself,
"That must have been the sun!"

* * *

But how he set, I know not.
There seemed a purple stile
Which little yellow boys and girls
Were climbing all the while

Till when they reached the other side,
A dominie in gray
Put gently up the evening bars,
And led the flock away.

Hen

by Mother Goose

Hen.
Cock, cock, cock, cock,
I've laid an egg,
Am I to gang ba-are-foot?
Cock.
Hen, hen, hen, hen,
I've been up and down,
To every shop in town,
And cannot find a shoe
To fit your foot,
If I'd crow my hea-art out.

[To be said very quickly, except the last two words in each verse, which are to be "screamed" out.]

Hope

by Emily Dickinson

Hope is the thing with feathers
That perches in the soul,
And sings the tune without the words,
And never stops at all,

And sweetest in the gale is heard;
And sore must be the storm
That could abash the little bird
That kept so many warm.

I've heard it in the chillest land,
And on the strangest sea;
Yet, never, in extremity,
It asked a crumb of me.

Daddy Longlegs

by Anne L. Huber

A big old daddy longlegs
Creeping on the wall,
I wish that he would go away,
I don't like him at all.

I know he will not hurt me,
But I don't want him here;
So get you gone, old daddy,
And don't come again so near.

Little Lad, Little Lad

by Mother Goose

Little lad, little lad,

Where were you born?

Far off in Lancashire, under a thorn,

Where they sup butter-milk

With a ram's horn;

And a pumpkin scoop'd,

With a yellow rim,

Is the bonny bowl they breakfast in.

There's a Certain Slant of Light

by Emily Dickinson

There's a certain slant of light,
On winter afternoons,
That oppresses, like the weight
Of cathedral tunes.

Heavenly hurt it gives us;
We can find no scar,
But internal difference
Where the meanings are.

None may teach it anything,
'Tis the seal despair,—
An imperial affliction
Sent us of the air.

When it comes, the landscape listens,
Shadows hold their breath;
When it goes, 'tis like the distance
On the look of death.

Sweet! Sweet!

by Louisa May Alcott

"Sweet! Sweet!
Come, come and eat,
Dear little girls
With yellow curls;
For here you'll find
Sweets to your mind.
On every tree
Sugar-plums you'll see;
In every dell
Grows the caramel.
Over every wall
Gum-drops fall;
Molasses flows
Where our river goes.
Under your feet
Lies sugar sweet;
Over your head

Grow almonds red.
Our lily and rose
Are not for the nose;
Our flowers we pluck
To eat or suck.
And, oh! what bliss
When two friends kiss,
For they honey sip
From lip to lip!
And all you meet,
In house or street,
At work or play,
Sweethearts are they.
So, little dear,
Pray feel no fear;
Go where you will;
Eat, eat your fill.
Here is a feast
From west to east;
And you can say,

Ere you go away,
'At last I stand
In dear Candy-land,
And no more can stuff;
For once I've enough.'
Sweet! Sweet!
Tweet! Tweet!
Tweedle-dee!
Tweedle-dee!"

Oh I Am So Happy

by Mother Goose

Oh I am so happy,
A little girl said,
As she sprang like a lark
From her low trundle bed.
It is morning, bright morning,
Good morning, Papa!
Oh give me one kiss,
For good morning, mamma!

Birds

by Ralph Waldo Emerson

Darlings of children and of bard,
Perfect kinds by vice unmarred,
All of worth and beauty set
Gems in Nature's cabinet;
These the fables she esteems
Reality most like to dreams.
Welcome back, you little nations,
Far-traveled in the south plantations;
Bring your music and rhythmic flight,
Your colors for our eyes' delight:
Freely nestle in our roof,
Weave your chamber weatherproof;
And your enchanting manners bring
And your autumnal gathering.
Exchange in conclave general
Greetings kind to each and all,
Conscious each of duty done
And unstain'd as the sun.

Pease Porridge
by Mother Goose

Pease porridge hot, pease porridge cold,
Pease porridge in the pot nine days old.

The Wild Birds Sing in the Orange Groves

by Louisa May Alcott

The wild birds sing in the orange groves,
And brightly bloom the flowers;
The fair earth smiles 'neath a summer sky
Through the joyous fleeting hours.
But oh! in the slave girl's lonely heart,
Sad thoughts and memories dwell,
And tears fall fast as she mournfully sings,
Home, dear home, farewell!

Though the chains they bind be all of flowers,
Where no hidden thorn may be,
Still the free heart sighs 'neath its fragrant bonds,
And pines for its liberty.
And sweet, sad thoughts of the joy now gone,
In the slave girl's heart shall dwell,
As she mournfully sings to her sighing harp,
Native land, native land, farewell!

The End of the Rainbow

by Sarah Morgan Bryan Piatt

May you go to find it? You must, I fear—
Ah, lighted young eyes, could I show you how!
"Is it past those lilies that look so near?"
It is past all flowers. Will you listen now?

The pretty new moons faded out of the sky,
The bees and butterflies out of the air;
And sweet wild songs would flutter and fly
Into wet dark leaves and the snow's white glare.

There were winds and shells full of lonesome
    cries;
There were lightnings and mists along the way;
And the deserts would glitter against my eyes,
Where the beautiful phantom-fountains play.

At last in a place very dusty and bare,
Some little dead birds I had petted to sing,

Some little dead flowers I had gathered to wear,
Some withered thorns, and an empty ring.

Lay scattered. My fairy story is told.
(It does not please her,—she has not smiled.)
What is it you say?—"Did I find the gold?"
Why, I found the End of the Rainbow, child!

Our Club

by Carolyn Wells

We're going to have the mostest fun!
　It's going to be a club;
And no one can belong to it
　But Dot and me and Bub.

We thought we'd have a Reading Club,
　But couldn't 'cause, you see,
Not one of us knows how to read—
　Not Dot nor Bub nor me.

And then we said a Sewing Club,
　But thought we'd better not;
'Cause none of us knows how to sew—
　Not me nor Bub nor Dot.

And so it's just a Playing Club,
　We play till time for tea;

And, oh, we have the bestest times!
   Just Dot and Bub and me.

One, Two—Buckle My Shoe

by Mother Goose

One, Two—buckle my shoe;
Three, Four—open the door;
Five, Six—pick up sticks;
Seven, Eight—lay them straight;
Nine, Ten—a good fat hen;
Eleven, Twelve—I hope you're well.
Thirteen, Fourteen—draw the curtain;
Fifteen, Sixteen—the maid's in the kitchen;
Seventeen, Eighteen—she's in waiting.
Nineteen, Twenty—my stomach's empty.

Sonnet XVII

by William Shakespeare

Who will believe my verse in time to come,

If it were fill'd with your most high deserts?

Though yet heaven knows it is but as a tomb

Which hides your life, and shows not half your
parts.

If I could write the beauty of your eyes,

And in fresh numbers number all your graces,

The age to come would say "This poet lies;

Such heavenly touches ne'er touch'd earthly
faces."

So should my papers, yellow'd with their age,

Be scorn'd, like old men of less truth than tongue,

And your true rights be term'd a poet's rage

And stretched meter of an antique song:

But were some child of yours alive that time,

You should live twice,—in it, and in my rhyme.

A Bicycle Built for Two

by Carolyn Wells

There was an ambitious young eel
Who determined to ride on a wheel;
    But try as he might,
    He couldn't ride right,
In spite of his ardor and zeal.

If he sat on the saddle to ride
His tail only pedaled one side;
    And I'm sure you'll admit
    That an eel couldn't sit
On a bicycle saddle astride.

Or if he hung over the top,
He could go, but he never could stop;
    For of course it is clear
    He had no way to steer,
And under the wheel he would flop.

His neighbor, observing the fun,
Said, "I think that the thing can be done,
    If you'll listen to me,
    You'll quickly agree
That two heads are better than one.

"And this is my project, old chap,
Around our two waists I will wrap
    This beautiful belt
    Of bottle-green felt
And fasten it firm with a strap."

This done, with a dignified mien
The two squirmed up on the machine,
    And rode gaily away,
    Or at least, so they say,
Who witnessed the wonderful scene.

A Farm-Picture

by Walt Whitman

Through the ample open door of the peaceful
country barn,

A sun-lit pasture field, with cattle and horses
feeding;

And haze, and vista, and the far horizon, fading
away.

Sonnet LIX

by William Shakespeare

If there be nothing new, but that which is
Hath been before, how are our brains beguil'd,
Which laboring for invention bear amiss
The second burthen of a former child!
O! that record could with a backward look,
Even of five hundred courses of the sun,
Show me your image in some antique book,
Since mind at first in character was done!
That I might see what the old world could say
To this composed wonder of your frame;
Wh'r we are mended, or wh'r better they,
Or whether revolution be the same.
O! sure I am the wits of former days,
To subjects worse have given admiring praise.

Jack and Jill

by Mother Goose

Jack and Jill went up the hill,

To draw a pail of water;

Jack fell down and broke his crown

And Jill came tumbling after.

A Riddle Song

by Walt Whitman

That which eludes this verse and any verse,

Unheard by sharpest ear, unform'd in clearest
eye or cunningest mind,

Nor lore nor fame, nor happiness nor wealth,

And yet the pulse of every heart and life
throughout the world incessantly,

Which you and I and all pursuing ever ever miss,

Open but still a secret, the real of the real, an
illusion,

Costless, vouchsafed to each, yet never man the
owner,

Which poets vainly seek to put in rhyme,
historians in prose,

Which sculptor never chisel'd yet, nor painter
painted,

Which vocalist never sung, nor orator nor actor
ever utter'd,

Invoking here and now I challenge for my song.

Indifferently, 'mid public, private haunts, in
  solitude,

Behind the mountain and the wood,

Companion of the city's busiest streets, through
  the assemblage,

It and its radiations constantly glide.

In looks of fair unconscious babes,

Or strangely in the coffin'd dead,

Or show of breaking dawn or stars by night,

As some dissolving delicate film of dreams,

Hiding yet lingering.

Two little breaths of words comprising it.

Two words, yet all from first to last comprised
  in it.

How ardently for it!

How many ships have sail'd and sunk for it!

How many travelers started from their homes
  and ne'er return'd!

How much of genius boldly staked and lost for it!

What countless stores of beauty, love, ventur'd
for it!

How all superbest deeds since Time began are
traceable to it—and shall be to the end!

How all heroic martyrdoms to it!

How, justified by it, the horrors, evils, battles of
the earth!

How the bright fascinating lambent flames of it,
in every age and land, have drawn men's eyes,

Rich as a sunset on the Norway coast, the sky,
the islands, and the cliffs,

Or midnight's silent glowing northern lights
unreachable.

Haply God's riddle it, so vague and yet so certain,

The soul for it, and all the visible universe for it,

And heaven at last for it.

Sweep, Sweep

by Mother Goose

Sweep, sweep,

Chimney sweep,

From the bottom to the top,

Sweep all up,

Chimney sweep,

From the bottom to the top.

Climb by rope,

Or climb by ladder,

Without either

I'll climb farther.

Mending Wall

by Robert Frost

Something there is that doesn't love a wall,
That sends the frozen-ground-swell under it,
And spills the upper boulders in the sun;
And makes gaps even two can pass abreast.
The work of hunters is another thing:
I have come after them and made repair
Where they have left not one stone on a stone,
But they would have the rabbit out of hiding,
To please the yelping dogs. The gaps I mean,
No one has seen them made or heard them made,
But at spring mending-time we find them there.
I let my neighbor know beyond the hill;
And on a day we meet to walk the line
And set the wall between us once again.
We keep the wall between us as we go.
To each the boulders that have fallen to each.
And some are loaves and some so nearly balls

We have to use a spell to make them balance:
"Stay where you are until our backs are turned!"
We wear our fingers rough with handling them.
Oh, just another kind of out-door game,
One on a side. It comes to little more:
There where it is we do not need the wall:
He is all pine and I am apple orchard.
My apple trees will never get across
And eat the cones under his pines, I tell him.
He only says, "Good fences make good
    neighbors."
Spring is the mischief in me, and I wonder
If I could put a notion in his head:
"Why do they make good neighbors? Isn't it
Where there are cows? But here there are no
    cows.
Before I built a wall I'd ask to know
What I was walling in or walling out,
And to whom I was like to give offense.
Something there is that doesn't love a wall,
That wants it down." I could say "Elves" to him,

But it's not elves exactly, and I'd rather
He said it for himself. I see him there
Bringing a stone grasped firmly by the top
In each hand, like an old-stone savage armed.
He moves in darkness as it seems to me,
Not of woods only and the shade of trees.
He will not go behind his father's saying,
And he likes having thought of it so well
He says again, "Good fences make good
    neighbors."

Peter, Peter, Pumpkin Eater

by Mother Goose

Peter, Peter, pumpkin eater,
Had a wife and couldn't keep her;
He put her in a pumpkin shell,
And then he kept her very well.
Peter, Peter, pumpkin eater,
Had another and didn't love her;
Peter learnt to read and spell,
And then he loved her very well.

Sonnet XCVI

by William Shakespeare

Some say thy fault is youth, some wantonness;
Some say thy grace is youth and gentle sport;
Both grace and faults are lov'd of more and less:
Thou mak'st faults graces that to thee resort.
As on the finger of a throned queen
The basest jewel will be well esteem'd,
So are those errors that in thee are seen
To truths translated, and for true things deem'd.
How many lambs might the stern wolf betray,
If like a lamb he could his looks translate!
How many gazers mightst thou lead away,
If thou wouldst use the strength of all thy state!
    But do not so; I love thee in such sort,
    As, thou being mine, mine is thy good report.

Milk-Man

by Mother Goose

Milk-man, milk-man, where have you been?
In Buttermilk channel up to my chin,
I spilt my milk, and I spoilt my clothes,
And got a long icicle hung to my nose.

Daisies

by Frank Dempster Sherman

At evening when I go to bed
I see the stars shine overhead.
They are the little daisies white
That dot the meadow of the night.

And often while I'm dreaming so,
Across the sky the moon will go.
It is a lady, sweet and fair,
Who comes to gather daisies there.

For, when at morning I arise,
There's not a star left in the skies,
She's picked them all
and dropped them down
Into the meadows of the town.

Signs of Spring

by Eudora Stone Bumstead

Breezes soft are blowing, blowing
   O'er the lea;
And the little flowers are growing,
   Fair to see.
And the grass is springing, springing,
   'Neath our feet;
And the early birds are singing,
   Clear and sweet.
Little lambs are racing, racing
   All the day;
And the warm bright sunbeams chasing
   Clouds away.
Busy bees are humming, humming
   'Mong the flowers.
Clouds are shifting—rain is coming—
   April showers.

Sonnet XXI

by William Shakespeare

So is it not with me as with that Muse,
Stirr'd by a painted beauty to his verse,
Who heaven itself for ornament doth use
And every fair with his fair doth rehearse;
Making a couplement of proud compare.
With sun and moon, with earth and sea's rich
    gems,
With April's first-born flowers, and all things
    rare,
That heaven's air in this huge rondure hems.
O! let me, true in love, but truly write,
And then believe me, my love is as fair
As any mother's child, though not so bright
As those gold candles fix'd in heaven's air:
    Let them say more that like of hearsay well;
    I will not praise that purpose not to sell.

Contrary Mary

by Mother Goose

Mistress Mary, quite contrary,
How does your garden grow?
With silver bells and cockle shells,
And maidens all in a row.

Sonnet CV

by William Shakespeare

Let not my love be call'd idolatry,
Nor my beloved as an idol show,
Since all alike my songs and praises be
To one, of one, still such, and ever so.
Kind is my love to-day, to-morrow kind,
Still constant in a wondrous excellence;
Therefore my verse to constancy confin'd,
One thing expressing, leaves out difference.
"Fair, kind, and true," is all my argument,
"Fair, kind, and true," varying to other words;
And in this change is my invention spent,
Three themes in one, which wondrous scope
    affords.
    Fair, kind, and true, have often liv'd alone,
    Which three till now, never kept seat in one.

Hunger

by Emily Dickinson

I had been hungry all the years;
My noon had come, to dine;
I, trembling, drew the table near,
And touched the curious wine.

'Twas this on tables I had seen,
When turning, hungry, lone,
I looked in windows, for the wealth
I could not hope to own.

I did not know the ample bread,
'Twas so unlike the crumb
The birds and I had often shared
In Nature's dining-room.

The plenty hurt me, 'twas so new,—
Myself felt ill and odd,

As berry of a mountain bush
Transplanted to the road.

Nor was I hungry; so I found
That hunger was a way
Of persons outside windows,
The entering takes away.

Hark! Hark! The Dogs Do Bark

by Mother Goose

Hark! hark! the dogs do bark,
The beggars have come to town;
Some in rags, and some in tags,
And some in velvet gowns.

The Robin Is the One

by Emily Dickinson

The robin is the one
That interrupts the morn
With hurried, few, express reports
When March is scarcely on.

The robin is the one
That overflows the noon
With her cherubic quantity,
An April but begun.

The robin is the one
That speechless from her nest
Submits that home and certainty
And sanctity are best.

A Song from the Suds

by Louisa May Alcott

Queen of my tub, I merrily sing,
　　While the white foam raises high,
And sturdily wash, and rinse, and wring,
　　And fasten the clothes to dry;
Then out in the free fresh air they swing,
　　Under the sunny sky.

I wish we could wash from our hearts and our souls
　　The stains of the week away,
And let water and air by their magic make
　　Ourselves as pure as they;
Then on the earth there would be indeed
　　A glorious washing day!

Along the path of a useful life
　　Will heart's-ease ever bloom;
The busy mind has no time to think

Of sorrow, or care, or gloom;
And anxious thoughts may be swept away
    As we busily wield a broom.

I am glad a task to me is given
    To labor at day by day;
For it brings me health, and strength, and hope,
    And I cheerfully learn to say,—
"Head, you may think; heart, you may feel;
    But hand, you shall work always!"

Children

by Henry Wadsworth Longfellow

Come to me, O ye children!
  For I hear you at your play,
And the questions that perplexed me
  Have vanished quite away.

Ye open the eastern windows,
  That look towards the sun,
Where thoughts are singing swallows
  And the brooks of morning run.

In your hearts are the birds and the sunshine,
  In your thoughts the brooklet's flow,
But in mine is the wind of Autumn
  And the first fall of the snow.

Ah! what would the world be to us
  If the children were no more?

We should dread the desert behind us
  Worse than the dark before.

What the leaves are to the forest,
  With light and air for food,
Ere their sweet and tender juices
  Have been hardened into wood,—

That to the world are children;
  Through them it feels the glow
Of a brighter and sunnier climate
  Than reaches the trunks below.

Come to me, O ye children!
  And whisper in my ear
What the birds and the winds are singing
  In your sunny atmosphere.

For what are all our contrivings,
  And the wisdom of our books,

When compared with your caresses,
  And the gladness of your looks?

Ye are better than all the ballads
  That ever were sung or said;
For ye are living poems,
  And all the rest are dead.

The Lion and the Unicorn

by Mother Goose

The lion and the Unicorn
Were fighting for the crown—
The lion beat the unicorn
All about the town.
Some gave them white bread,
And some gave them brown,
Some gave them plum-cake,
And sent them out of town.

To the Moon
by Percy Bysshe Shelley

I

Art thou pale for weariness
Of climbing heaven and gazing on the earth,
Wandering companionless
Among the stars that have a different birth,—
And ever changing, like a joyless eye
That finds no object worth its constancy?

II

Thou chosen sister of the Spirit,
That gazes on thee till in thee it pities . . .

Two Blackbirds

by Mother Goose

There were two blackbirds sitting on a hill,
One name Jack, and the other name Jill;
Fly away, Jack—fly away, Jill,
Come again, Jack—come again, Jill.

The Ant

by Oliver Herford

My child, ob-serve the use-ful Ant,
How hard she works each day;
She works as hard as ad-a-mant
(That's very hard, they say).
She has no time to gal-li-vant;
She has no time to play.
Let Fi-do chase his tail all day;
Let Kit-ty play at tag;
She has no time to throw away,
She has no tail to wag;
She scurries round from morn till night;
She nev-er, nev-er sleeps;
She seiz-es ev-er-y-thing in sight,
She drags it home with all her might,
And all she takes she keeps.

At Home

by Emily Dickinson

The night was wide, and furnished scant
With but a single star,
That often as a cloud it met
Blew out itself for fear.

The wind pursued the little bush,
And drove away the leaves
November left; then clambered up
And fretted in the eaves.

No squirrel went abroad;
A dog's belated feet
Like intermittent plush were heard
Adown the empty street.

To feel if blinds be fast,
And closer to the fire

Her little rocking-chair to draw,
And shiver for the poor,

The housewife's gentle task.
"How pleasanter," said she
Unto the sofa opposite,
"The sleet than May—no thee!"

Sonnet CXXX

by William Shakespeare

My mistress' eyes are nothing like the sun;
Coral is far more red, than her lips red:
If snow be white, why then her breasts are dun;
If hairs be wires, black wires grow on her head.
I have seen roses damask'd, red and white,
But no such roses see I in her cheeks;
And in some perfumes is there more delight
Than in the breath that from my mistress reeks.
I love to hear her speak,—yet well I know
That music hath a far more pleasing sound:
I grant I never saw a goddess go,—
My mistress, when she walks, treads on the
    ground:
    And yet by heaven, I think my love as rare,
    As any she belied with false compare.

Answer to a Child's Question

by Samuel Taylor Coleridge

Do you ask what the birds say? The sparrow, the
dove,

The linnet and thrush say, "I love and I love!"

In the winter they're silent—the wind is so
strong;

What it says, I don't know, but it sings a loud
song.

But green leaves, and blossoms, and sunny warm
weather,

And singing, and loving—all come back together.

But the lark is so brimful of gladness and love,

The green fields below him, the blue sky above,

That he sings, and he sings; and for ever sings
he—

"I love my love, and my love loves me!"

A Late Walk

by Robert Frost

When I go up through the mowing field,
    The headless aftermath,
Smooth-laid like thatch with the heavy dew,
    Half closes the garden path.

And when I come to the garden ground,
    The whir of sober birds
Up from the tangle of withered weeds
    Is sadder than any words.

A tree beside the wall stands bare,
    But a leaf that lingered brown,
Disturbed, I doubt not, by my thought,
    Comes softly rattling down.

I end not far from my going forth
    By picking the faded blue

Of the last remaining aster flower
To carry again to you.

News of the Day

by Mother Goose

What's the news of the day,
Good neighbor, I pray?
They say the balloon
Has gone up to the moon.

The Balloon of the Mind

by W. B. Yeats

Hands, do what you're bid:
Bring the balloon of the mind
That bellies and drags in the wind
Into its narrow shed.

Burs

by Mary Mapes Dodge

Dear me!
What shall it be?
Such sticky affairs
Did ever you see?
Let's make a basket,
Let's make a mat,
Let's make a tea-board,
Let's make a hat;
Let's make a cottage,
Windows and doors;
You do the roof,
And I'll do the floors.
Let's make a pancake,—
Stick 'em together;
See how they fasten
Close to each other!
Tied to one's heel

They would answer for spurs;
Ah, how we love 'em,
These comical burs!

The Storm

by Emily Dickinson

There came a wind like a bugle;
It quivered through the grass,
And a green chill upon the heat
So ominous did pass
We barred the windows and the doors,
As from an emerald ghost;
The doom's electric moccasin
That very instant passed.
On a strange mob of panting trees,
And fences fled away,
And rivers where the houses ran
The living looked that day.
The bell within the steeple wild
The flying tidings whirled.
How much can come
And much can go,
And yet abide the world!

When You Are Old
by W. B. Yeats

When you are old and grey and full of sleep,
And nodding by the fire, take down this book,
And slowly read, and dream of the soft look
Your eyes had once, and of their shadows deep;

How many loved your moments of glad grace,
And loved your beauty with love false or true,
But one man loved the pilgrim soul in you,
And loved the sorrows of your changing face;

And bending down beside the glowing bars,
Murmur, a little sadly, how love fled
And paced upon the mountains overhead
And hid his face amid a crowd of stars.

Hogs in the Garden

by Mother Goose

Hogs in the garden, catch 'em, Towser;
Cows in the corn-field, run boys, run,
Cats in the cream-pot, run girls, run girls;
Fire on the mountains, run boys, run.

Sonnet XXXVII

by William Shakespeare

As a decrepit father takes delight
To see his active child do deeds of youth,
So I, made lame by Fortune's dearest spite,
Take all my comfort of thy worth and truth;
For whether beauty, birth, or wealth, or wit,
Or any of these all, or all, or more,
Entitled in thy parts, do crowned sit,
I make my love engrafted, to this store:
So then I am not lame, poor, nor despis'd,
Whilst that this shadow doth such substance give
That I in thy abundance am suffic'd,
And by a part of all thy glory live.
    Look what is best, that best I wish in thee:
    This wish I have; then ten times happy me!

Secrets

by Emily Dickinson

The skies can't keep their secret!
They tell it to the hills—
The hills just tell the orchards—
And they the daffodils!

A bird, by chance, that goes that way
Soft overheard the whole.
If I should bribe the little bird,
Who knows but she would tell?

I think I won't, however,
It's finer not to know;
If summer were an axiom,
What sorcery had snow?

So keep your secret, Father!
I would not, if I could,

Know what the sapphire fellows do,
In your new-fashioned world!

My Voice
by Oscar Wilde

Within the restless, hurried, modern world
    We took our hearts' full pleasure—You and I,
And now the white sails of our ships are furled,
    And spent the lading of our argosy.

Wherefore my cheeks before their time are wan,
    For very weeping is my gladness fled,
Sorrow hath paled my lip's vermilion
    And Ruin draws the curtains of my bed.

But all this crowded life has been to thee
    No more than lyre, or lute, or subtle spell
Of viols, or the music of the sea
    That sleeps, a mimic echo, in the shell.

Sonnet XLIII

by William Shakespeare

When most I wink, then do mine eyes best see,

For all the day they view things unrespected;

But when I sleep, in dreams they look on thee,

And darkly bright, are bright in dark directed.

Then thou, whose shadow shadows doth make
bright,

How would thy shadow's form form happy show

To the clear day with thy much clearer light,

When to unseeing eyes thy shade shines so!

How would, I say, mine eyes be blessed made

By looking on thee in the living day,

When in dead night thy fair imperfect shade

Through heavy sleep on sightless eyes doth stay!

    All days are nights to see till I see thee,

    And nights bright days when dreams do show
thee me.

I Had a Little Doll

by Mother Goose

I had a little doll,
The prettiest ever seen,
She washed me the dishes,
And kept the house clean.
She went to the mill
To fetch me some flour,
And always got it home
In less than an hour;
She baked me my bread,
She brewed me my ale,
She sat by the fire
And told many a fine tale.

She Walks in Beauty
by Lord Byron

She walks in beauty, like the night
Of cloudless climes and starry skies;
And all that's best of dark and bright
Meet in her aspect and her eyes;
Thus mellowed to that tender light
Which heaven to gaudy day denies.

One shade the more, one ray the less,
Had half impaired the nameless grace
Which waves in every raven tress,
Or softly lightens o'er her face;
Where thoughts serenely sweet express,
How pure, how dear their dwelling-place.

And on that cheek, and o'er that brow,
So soft, so calm, yet eloquent,
The smiles that win, the tints that glow,

But tell of days in goodness spent,
A mind at peace with all below,
A heart whose love is innocent!

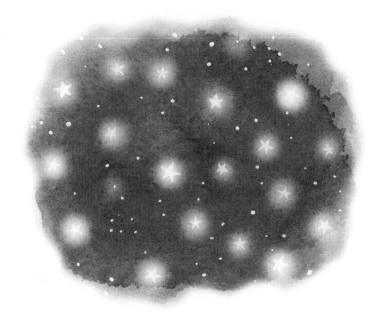

Play

by William Carlos Williams

Subtle, clever brain, wiser than I am,
By what devious means do you contrive
To remain idle? Teach me, O master.

There Was a Piper Had a Cow

by Mother Goose

There was a Piper had a Cow,

And he had naught to give her,

He pull'd out his pipes and play'd her a tune,

And bade the cow consider.

The cow considered very well,

And gave the piper a penny,

And bade him play the other tune,

"Corn rigs are bonny."

Sonnet LX

by William Shakespeare

Like as the waves make towards the pebbled
  shore,
So do our minutes hasten to their end;
Each changing place with that which goes before,
In sequent toil all forward do contend.
Nativity, once in the main of light,
Crawls to maturity, wherewith being crown'd,
Crooked eclipses 'gainst his glory fight,
And Time that gave doth now his gift confound.
Time doth transfix the flourish set on youth
And delves the parallels in beauty's brow,
Feeds on the rarities of nature's truth,
And nothing stands but for his scythe to mow:
    And yet to times in hope, my verse shall stand.
    Praising thy worth, despite his cruel hand.

Pussy Cat, Pussy Cat
by Mother Goose

Pussy cat, pussy cat, where have you been?

I've been to London to see the Queen.

Pussy cat, pussy cat, what did you there?

I frightened a little mouse under the chair.

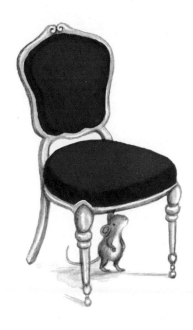

The Road Not Taken

by Robert Frost

Two roads diverged in a yellow wood,
And sorry I could not travel both
And be one traveler, long I stood
And looked down one as far as I could
To where it bent in the undergrowth;

Then took the other, as just as fair,
And having perhaps the better claim,
Because it was grassy and wanted wear;
Though as for that the passing there
Had worn them really about the same,

And both that morning equally lay
In leaves no step had trodden black.
Oh, I kept the first for another day!
Yet knowing how way leads on to way,
I doubted if I should ever come back.

I shall be telling this with a sigh
Somewhere ages and ages hence:
Two roads diverged in a wood, and I—
I took the one less traveled by,
And that has made all the difference.

The Ecchoing Green

by William Blake

The sun does arise,
And make happy the skies.
The merry bells ring
To welcome the Spring.
The sky-lark and thrush,
The birds of the bush,
Sing louder around,
To the bells' cheerful sound.
While our sports shall be seen
On the Ecchoing Green.

Old John, with white hair
Does laugh away care,
Sitting under the oak,
Among the old folk,
They laugh at our play,
And soon they all say.

'Such, such were the joys.
When we all girls & boys,
In our youth-time were seen,
On the Ecchoing Green.'

Till the little ones weary
No more can be merry
The sun does descend,
And our sports have an end:
Round the laps of their mothers,
Many sisters and brothers,
Like birds in their nest,
Are ready for rest;
And sport no more seen,
On the darkening Green.

Snow-Flakes

by Mary Mapes Dodge

Whenever a snow-flake leaves the sky,
　　It turns and turns to say "Good-bye!
　　Good-bye, dear clouds, so cool and gray!"
　　Then lightly travels on its way.

And when a snow-flake finds a tree,
　　"Good-day!" it says—"Good-day to thee!
　　Thou art so bare, and lonely, dear,
　　I'll rest and call my comrades here."

But when a snow-flake, brave and meek,
　　Lights on a rosy maiden's cheek,
　　It starts—"How warm and soft the day!
　　'T is summer!"—and it melts away.

Good King Arthur
by Mother Goose

When good King Arthur ruled his land
He was a goodly king;
He stole three pecks of barley meal
To make a bag-pudding.
A bag-pudding the king did make,
And stuff'd it well with plums;
And in it put great lumps of fat,
As big as my two thumbs.
The king and queen did eat thereof,
And noblemen beside;
And what they could not eat that night,
The queen next morning fried.

In the Garden

by Emily Dickinson

A bird came down the walk:
He did not know I saw;
He bit an angle-worm in halves
And ate the fellow, raw.

And then he drank a dew
From a convenient grass,
And then hopped sidewise to the wall
To let a beetle pass.

He glanced with rapid eyes
That hurried all abroad,—
They looked like frightened beads, I thought;
He stirred his velvet head

Like one in danger; cautious,
I offered him a crumb,

And he unrolled his feathers
And rowed him softer home

Than oars divide the ocean,
Too silver for a seam,
Or butterflies, off banks of noon,
Leap, plashless, as they swim.

Wynken, Blynken, and Nod
by Eugene Field

Wynken, Blynken, and Nod one night
  Sailed off in a wooden shoe,
Sailed on a river of crystal light
  Into a sea of dew.
"Where are you going, and what do you wish?"
  The old moon asked the three;—
"We have come to fish for the herring-fish
  That live in this beautiful sea;
  Nets of silver and gold have we,"
      Said Wynken,
      Blynken,
      And Nod.

The old moon laughed and sang a song,
  As they rocked in the wooden shoe;
And the wind that sped them all night long
  Ruffled the waves of dew;
The little stars were the herring-fish

That lived in the beautiful sea;—
"Now cast your nets wherever you wish,
  Never afraid are we!"
  So cried the stars to the fishermen three,
        Wynken,
        Blynken,
        And Nod.

All night long their nets they threw
  To the stars in the twinkling foam,—
Then down from the skies came the wooden shoe,
  Bringing the fishermen home:
'Twas all so pretty a sail, it seemed
  As if it could not be;
And some folk thought 'twas a dream they'd
    dreamed
  Of sailing that beautiful sea;—
  But I shall name you the fishermen three:
        Wynken,
        Blynken,
        And Nod.

Wynken and Blynken are two little eyes,
  And Nod is a little head,
And the wooden shoe that sailed the skies
  Is a wee one's trundle bed;
So shut your eyes while Mother sings
  Of wonderful sights that be,
And you shall see the beautiful things
  As you rock in the misty sea.
  Where the old shoe rocked the fishermen
    three;—
      Wynken,
      Blynken,
      And Nod.

Little Tommy Tucker

by Mother Goose

Little Tommy Tucker,
Sing for your supper:
What shall I sing?
White bread and butter.
How shall I cut it
Without any knife?
How shall I marry
Without any wife?

Sonnet LXXVIII

by William Shakespeare

So oft have I invoked thee for my Muse,
And found such fair assistance in my verse
As every alien pen hath got my use
And under thee their poesy disperse.
Thine eyes, that taught the dumb on high to sing
And heavy ignorance aloft to fly,
Have added feathers to the learned's wing
And given grace a double majesty.
Yet be most proud of that which I compile,
Whose influence is thine, and born of thee:
In others' works thou dost but mend the style,
And arts with thy sweet graces graced be;
    But thou art all my art, and dost advance
    As high as learning, my rude ignorance.

The Lost Thought

by Emily Dickinson

I felt a clearing in my mind
   As if my brain had split;
I tried to match it, seam by seam,
   But could not make them fit.

The thought behind I strove to join
   Unto the thought before,
But sequence raveled out of reach
   Like balls upon a floor.

Mary's Lamb

by Sarah Josepha Hale

Mary had a little lamb,
Its fleece was white as snow,
And everywhere that Mary went
The lamb was sure to go;
He followed her to school one day—
That was against the rule,
It made the children laugh and play,
To see a lamb at school.

And so the Teacher turned him out,
But still he lingered near,
And waited patiently about,
Till Mary did appear;
And then he ran to her, and laid
His head upon her arm,
As if he said—"I'm not afraid—
You'll keep me from all harm."

"What makes the lamb love Mary so?"
The eager children cry—
"O, Mary loves the lamb, you know,"
The Teacher did reply;—
"And you each gentle animal
In confidence may bind,
And make them follow at your call,
If you are always kind."

To My Father on His Birthday

by Elizabeth Barrett Browning

Amidst the days of pleasant mirth,
That throw their halo round our earth;
Amidst the tender thoughts that rise
To call bright tears to happy eyes;
Amidst the silken words that move
To syllable the names we love;
There glides no day of gentle bliss
More soothing to the heart than this!
No thoughts of fondness e'er appear
More fond, than those I write of here!
No name can e'er on tablet shine,
My father! more beloved than thine!
'Tis sweet, adown the shady past,
A lingering look of love to cast—
Back th' enchanted world to call,
That beamed around us first of all;

And walk with Memory fondly o'er
The paths where Hope had been before—
Sweet to receive the sylphic sound
That breathes in tenderness around,
Repeating to the listening ear
The names that made our childhood dear—
For parted Joy, like Echo, kind,
Will leave her dulcet voice behind,
To tell, amidst the magic air,
How oft she smiled and lingered there.

Problems

by Emily Dickinson

Bring me the sunset in a cup,
Reckon the morning's flagons up,
   And say how many dew;
Tell me how far the morning leaps,
Tell me what time the weaver sleeps
   Who spun the breadths of blue!

Write me how many notes there be
In the new robin's ecstasy
   Among astonished boughs;
How many trips the tortoise makes,
How many cups the bee partakes,—
   The debauchee of dews!

Also, who laid the rainbow's piers,
Also, who leads the docile spheres
   By withes of supple blue?

Whose fingers string the stalactite,
Who counts the wampum of the night,
   To see that none is due?

Who built this little Alban house
And shut the windows down so close
   My spirit cannot see?
Who'll let me out some gala day,
With implements to fly away,
   Passing pomposity?

Mary Had a Pretty Bird

by Mother Goose

Mary had a pretty bird,

Feathers bright and yellow,

Slender legs, upon my word

He was a pretty fellow.

The sweetest notes he always sung,

Which much delighted Mary,

And often where the cage was hung,

She stood to hear Canary.

Sonnet CXLVIII

by William Shakespeare

O me! what eyes hath Love put in my head,
Which have no correspondence with true sight;
Or, if they have, where is my judgment fled,
That censures falsely what they see aright?
If that be fair whereon my false eyes dote,
What means the world to say it is not so?
If it be not, then love doth well denote
Love's eye is not so true as all men's: no,
How can it? O! how can Love's eye be true,
That is so vexed with watching and with tears?
No marvel then, though I mistake my view;
The sun itself sees not, till heaven clears.
 O cunning Love! with tears thou keep'st me
  blind,
 Lest eyes well-seeing thy foul faults should
  find.

Love and Friendship

by Emily Brontë

Love is like the wild rose-briar,
Friendship like the holly-tree—
The holly is dark when the rose-briar blooms
But which will bloom most constantly?

The wild rose-briar is sweet in spring,
Its summer blossoms scent the air;
Yet wait till winter comes again
And who will call the wild-briar fair?

Then scorn the silly rose-wreath now
And deck thee with the holly's sheen,
That when December blights thy brow
He still may leave thy garland green.

Leap Year Poem

by Mother Goose

Thirty days hath September,
April, June and November.
All the rest have thirty-one,
Excepting February alone,
And that has twenty-eight days clear
And twenty-nine in each leap year.

Friends

by Emily Dickinson

Are friends delight or pain?
Could bounty but remain
  Riches were good.

But if they only stay
Bolder to fly away,
  Riches are sad.

The Reason Why

by Gertrude Heath

To-day the first June rose bloomed out,
Down by the daisies and clover;
All a-tremble, with leaves a-pout,
Buttercups bending over.

"Sweet, so sweet!" the butterfly said,
"Rose in your rustic splendor!"
And honey-bees lingered over her head,
Murmuring love-words tender.

Sweet, little, blushing, wayside Rose,
Tell me what is the reason
All of your brothers and sisters sleep,
You are the first of the season?

All a-blushing the little Rose said:
"I know they can not have missed me!

I waked this morning (she hung her head)
Because a honey-bee kissed me!"

Waiting

by William Carlos Williams

When I am alone I am happy.
The air is cool. The sky is
flecked and splashed and wound
with color. The crimson phalloi
of the sassafras leaves
hang crowded before me
in shoals on the heavy branches.
When I reach my doorstep
I am greeted by
the happy shrieks of my children
and my heart sinks.
I am crushed.

Are not my children as dear to me
as falling leaves or
must one become stupid
to grow older?

It seems much as if Sorrow
had tripped up my heels.
Let us see, let us see!
What did I plan to say to her
when it should happen to me
as it has happened now?

Little Jack Nory

by Mother Goose

Little Jack Nory
Told me a story
How he tried
Cock-horse to ride,
Sword and scabbard by his side,
Saddle, leaden spurs and switches,
His pocket tight
With cents all bright,
Marbles, tops, puzzles, props,
Now he's put in jacket and breeches.

The Wind

by Emily Dickinson

It's like the light,—
  A fashionless delight
It's like the bee,—
  A dateless melody.

It's like the woods,
  Private like breeze,
Phraseless, yet it stirs
  The proudest trees.

It's like the morning,—
  Best when it's done,—
The everlasting clocks
  Chime noon.

Humming-bird Song

by Frank Dempster Sherman

Humming-bird,
Not a word
Do you say;
Has your throat
No sweet note
To repay
Honest debts
It begets
When you go
On the wing
Pilfering
To and fro?

May be you
Whisper to
Bloom and leaf
On the vine

Secrets fine
In your brief
Calls on them,
Winged gem.
Not a word
You reply!
Off you fly,
Humming-bird!

The Land of Nod

by Robert Louis Stevenson

From breakfast on through all the day
At home among my friends I stay,
But every night I go abroad
Afar into the land of Nod.

All by myself I have to go,
With none to tell me what to do—
All alone beside the streams
And up the mountain-sides of dreams.

The strangest things are there for me,
Both things to eat and things to see,
And many frightening sights abroad
Till morning in the land of Nod.

Try as I like to find the way,
I never can get back by day,
Nor can remember plain and clear
The curious music that I hear.

Sonnet XLIX

by William Shakespeare

Against that time, if ever that time come,
When I shall see thee frown on my defects,
When as thy love hath cast his utmost sum,
Call'd to that audit by advis'd respects;
Against that time when thou shalt strangely pass,
And scarcely greet me with that sun, thine eye,
When love, converted from the thing it was,
Shall reasons find of settled gravity;
Against that time do I ensconce me here,
Within the knowledge of mine own desert,
And this my hand, against my self uprear,
To guard the lawful reasons on thy part:
    To leave poor me thou hast the strength of laws,
    Since why to love I can allege no cause.

To Make a Prairie

by Emily Dickinson

To make a prairie it takes a clover and one bee,—
One clover, and a bee,
And revery.
The revery alone will do
If bees are few.

Cock a Doodle Doo

by Mother Goose

Cock a doodle doo,

My dame has lost her shoe;

My master's lost his fiddlestick,

And knows not what to do.

Lullaby

by Louisa May Alcott

Now the day is done,
Now the shepherd sun
Drives his white flocks from the sky;
Now the flowers rest
On their mother's breast,
Hushed by her low lullaby.

Now the glowworms glance,
Now the fireflies dance,
Under fern-boughs green and high;
And the western breeze
To the forest trees
Chants a tuneful lullaby.

Now 'mid shadows deep
Falls blessed sleep,
Like dew from the summer sky;

And the whole earth dreams,
In the moon's soft beams,
While night breathes a lullaby.

Now, birdlings, rest,
In your wind-rocked nest,
Unscared by the owl's shrill cry;
For with folded wings
Little Brier swings,
And singeth your lullaby.

Baa, Baa, Black Sheep

by Mother Goose

Baa, baa, black sheep, have you any wool?

Yes, marry have I, three bags full,

One for my master, and one for my dame,

And one for the little boy who lives in the lane.

Late, Late, So Late

by Alfred Lord Tennyson

Late, late, so late! and dark the night and chill!
Late, late, so late! but we can enter still.
Too late, too late! ye cannot enter now.

No light had we: for that we do repent;
And learning this, the bridegroom will relent.
Too late, too late! ye cannot enter now.

No light: so late! and dark and chill the night!
O, let us in, that we may find the light!
Too late, too late: ye cannot enter now.

Have we not heard the bridegroom is so sweet?
O, let us in, tho' late, to kiss his feet!
No, no, too late! ye cannot enter now.

Sonnet LXXVII
by William Shakespeare

Thy glass will show thee how thy beauties wear,
Thy dial how thy precious minutes waste;
These vacant leaves thy mind's imprint will bear,
And of this book, this learning mayst thou taste.
The wrinkles which thy glass will truly show
Of mouthed graves will give thee memory;
Thou by thy dial's shady stealth mayst know
Time's thievish progress to eternity.
Look! what thy memory cannot contain,
Commit to these waste blanks, and thou shalt
    find
Those children nursed, deliver'd from thy brain,
To take a new acquaintance of thy mind.
    These offices, so oft as thou wilt look,
    Shall profit thee and much enrich thy book.

Little Boy Blue

by Mother Goose

Little boy blue, come blow your horn,
The sheep's in the meadow, the cow's in the corn,
What! is this the way you mind your sheep,
Under the haycock fast asleep?

My Uncle Jehoshaphat

by Laura Elizabeth Howe Richards

My Uncle Jehoshaphat had a pig,
A pig of high degree;
And he always wore a brown scratch wig,
Most beautiful for to see.

My Uncle Jehoshaphat loved this pig,
And the piggywig he loved him;
And they both jumped into the lake one day,
To see which best could swim.

My Uncle Jehoshaphat he swam up,
And the piggywig he swam down;
And so they both did win the prize,
Which same was a velvet gown.

My Uncle Jehoshaphat wore one half,
And piggywig wore the other;

And they both rode to town on the brindled calf,
To carry it home to its mother.

On the Grasshopper and Cricket

by John Keats

The poetry of earth is never dead:
  When all the birds are faint with the hot sun,
  And hide in cooling trees, a voice will run
From hedge to hedge about the new-mown
    mead;
That is the Grasshopper's—he takes the lead
  In summer luxury,—he has never done
  With his delights; for when tired out with fun
He rests at ease beneath some pleasant weed.
The poetry of earth is ceasing never:
  On a lone winter evening, when the frost
    Has wrought a silence, from the stove there
    shrills
The Cricket's song, in warmth increasing ever,
  And seems to one in drowsiness half lost,
    The Grasshopper's among some grassy hills.

Iris Flowers

by Mary McNeil Fenollosa

My mother let me go with her,
(I had been good all day),
To see the iris flowers that bloom
In gardens far away.

We walked and walked through hedges green,
Through rice-fields empty still,
To where we saw a garden gate
Beneath the farthest hill.

She pointed out the rows of "flowers";—I saw no
    planted things,
But white and purple butterflies
Tied down with silken strings.

They strained and fluttered in the breeze,
So eager to be free;

I begged the man to let them go,
But mother laughed at me.

She said that they could never rise,
Like birds, to heaven so blue.
But even mothers do not know
Some things that children do.

That night, the flowers untied themselves
And softly stole away,
To fly in sunshine round my dreams
Until the break of day.

There Was a Mad Man

by Mother Goose

There was a mad man,
And he had a mad wife,
And they lived all in a mad lane!
They had three children all at a birth,
And they too were mad every one.
The father was mad,
The mother was mad,
The children all mad beside;
And upon a mad horse they all of them got,
And madly away did ride.

The Lonely Street

by William Carlos Williams

School is over. It is too hot
to walk at ease. At ease
in light frocks they walk the streets
to while the time away.
They have grown tall. They hold
pink flames in their right hands.
In white from head to foot,
with sidelong, idle look—
in yellow, floating stuff,
black sash and stockings—touching their avid
mouths
with pink sugar on a stick—like a carnation
each holds in her hand—they mount the
lonely street.

An Alice Alphabet

by Carolyn Wells

A is for Alice a-dressing the Queen.

B is for Borogoves, mimsy and lean.

C is the Cheshire Cat, wearing a grin.

D is the Duchess who had a sharp chin.

E is the Eaglet who barred out long words.

F, the Flamingo, the queerest of birds.

G is the Gryphon, loquacious and gay.

H, Humpty Dumpty in gorgeous array.

I is for Insects with curious names.

J is the Jabberwock burbling with flames.

K is the King who was whizzed through the air.

L is the Lobster who sugared his hair.

M, the Mock Turtle, whose tears freely flowed.

N is for Nobody seen on the road.

O is for Oysters who trotted so quick.

P is the Puppy who played with a stick.

Q is the Queen who ran very fast.

R is the Rabbit who blew a great blast.

S is the Sheep, on her knitting intent.

T, Tweedledum, with his noisy lament.

U is the Unicorn, valiant in feud.

V is the Violet, saucy and rude.

W, the Walrus, addicted to chat.

X, Executioner, seeking the cat.

Y is the Youth Father William surveyed.

Z is the Zigzag the mouse's tail made.

Sonnet CXLIII

by William Shakespeare

Lo, as a careful housewife runs to catch
One of her feather'd creatures broke away,
Sets down her babe, and makes all swift dispatch
In pursuit of the thing she would have stay;
Whilst her neglected child holds her in chase,
Cries to catch her whose busy care is bent
To follow that which flies before her face,
Not prizing her poor infant's discontent;
So runn'st thou after that which flies from thee,
Whilst I thy babe chase thee afar behind;
But if thou catch thy hope, turn back to me,
And play the mother's part, kiss me, be kind;
   So will I pray that thou mayst have thy "Will,"
   If thou turn back and my loud crying still.

I Asked No Other Thing

by Emily Dickinson

I asked no other thing,
No other was denied.
I offered Being for it;
The mighty merchant smiled.

Brazil? He twirled a button,
Without a glance my way:
"But, madam, is there nothing else
That we can show to-day?"

To Market, to Market

by Mother Goose

To market, to market, to buy a penny bun,
Home again, home again, market is done.

Limits

by Ralph Waldo Emerson

Who knows this or that?
Hark in the wall to the rat:
Since the world was, he has gnawed;
Of his wisdom, of his fraud
What dost thou know?
In the wretched little beast
Is life and heart,
Child and parent,
Not without relation
To fruitful field and sun and moon.
What art thou? His wicked eye
Is cruel to thy cruelty.

The Man in the Wilderness

by Mother Goose

The man in the wilderness,

Asked me,

How many strawberries

Grew in the sea?

I answered him as I thought good,

As many red herrings

As grew in the wood.

The Tryst
by Father John B. Tabb

Potato was deep in the dark underground,
Tomato, above in the light.
The little Tomato was ruddy and round,
The little Potato was white.
And redder and redder she rounded above,
And paler and paler he grew,
And neither suspected a mutual love
Till they met in a Brunswick stew.

The City of Sleep

by Rudyard Kipling

Over the edge of the purple down,
　　Where the single lamplight gleams,
Know ye the road to the Merciful Town
　　That is hard by the Sea of Dreams—
Where the poor may lay their wrongs away,
　　And the sick may forget to weep?
But we—pity us! Oh, pity us!
　　We wakeful; ah, pity us!—
We must go back with Policeman Day—
　　Back from the City of Sleep!

Weary they turn from the scroll and crown,
　　Fetter and prayer and plough—
They that go up to the Merciful Town,
　　For her gates are closing now.
It is their right in the Baths of Night
　　Body and soul to steep,

But we—pity us! ah, pity us!
  We wakeful; oh, pity us!—
We must go back with Policeman Day—
  Back from the City of Sleep!

Over the edge of the purple down,
  Ere the tender dreams begin,
Look—we may look—at the Merciful Town,
  But we may not enter in!
Outcasts all, from her guarded wall
  Back to our watch we creep:
We—pity us! ah, pity us!
  We wakeful; ah, pity us!—
We that go back with Policeman Day—
  Back from the City of Sleep!

Dawn

by Emily Dickinson

When night is almost done,
And sunrise grows so near
That we can touch the spaces,
It's time to smooth the hair

And get the dimples ready,
And wonder we could care
For that old faded midnight
That frightened but an hour.

The Man in the Moon

by Mother Goose

The man in the moon came down too soon
To inquire the way to Norridge;
The man in the south, he burnt his mouth
With eating cold plum porridge.

Sonnet LXXXII

by William Shakespeare

I grant thou wert not married to my Muse,
And therefore mayst without attaint o'erlook
The dedicated words which writers use
Of their fair subject, blessing every book.
Thou art as fair in knowledge as in hue,
Finding thy worth a limit past my praise;
And therefore art enforced to seek anew
Some fresher stamp of the time-bettering days.
And do so, love; yet when they have devis'd,
What strained touches rhetoric can lend,
Thou truly fair, wert truly sympathiz'd
In true plain words, by thy true-telling friend;
 And their gross painting might be better us'd
 Where cheeks need blood; in thee it is abus'd.

Little Robin Redbreast

by Mother Goose

Little Robin Redbreast
Sat upon a tree,
Up went the Pussy Cat,
And down went he;

Down came Pussy Cat,
Away Robin ran,
Says little Robin Redbreast—
Catch me if you can.

Little Robin Redbreast
jumped upon a spade,
Pussy Cat jumped after him,
and then he was afraid.

Little Robin chirped and sung,
and what did Pussy say?

Pussy Cat said Mew, mew mew,—
and Robin flew away.

Now

by Robert Browning

Out of your whole life give but a moment!

All of your life that has gone before,

All to come after it,—so you ignore,

So you make perfect the present,—condense,

In a rapture of rage, for perfection's endowment,

Thought and feeling and soul and sense—

Merged in a moment which gives me at last

You around me for once, you beneath me, above
me—

Me—sure that despite of time future, time
past,—

This tick of our life-time's one moment you
love me!

How long such suspension may linger? Ah,
Sweet—

The moment eternal—just that and no more—

When ecstasy's utmost we clutch at the core

While cheeks burn, arms open, eyes shut and
lips meet!

When I Was a Little Boy, I Lived by Myself

by Mother Goose

When I was a little boy, I lived by myself,

And all the bread and cheese I got I put upon a shelf;

The rats and the mice, they made such a strife,

I was forced to go to London to buy me a wife.

The streets were so broad, and the lanes were so narrow.

I was forced to bring my wife home in a wheelbarrow;

The wheelbarrow broke, and my wife had a fall,

And down came the wheelbarrow, wife and all.

A Well

by Emily Dickinson

What mystery pervades a well!
  The water lives so far,
Like neighbor from another world
  Residing in a jar.

The grass does not appear afraid;
  I often wonder he
Can stand so close and look so bold
  At what is dread to me.

Related somehow they may be,—
  The sedge stands next the sea,
Where he is floorless, yet of fear
  No evidence gives he.

But nature is a stranger yet;
  The ones that cite her most

Have never passed her haunted house,
 Nor simplified her ghost.

To pity those that know her not
 Is helped by the regret
That those who know her, know her less
 The nearer her they get.

Sonnet CXXII

by William Shakespeare

Thy gift, thy tables, are within my brain
Full character'd with lasting memory,
Which shall above that idle rank remain,
Beyond all date; even to eternity:
Or, at the least, so long as brain and heart
Have faculty by nature to subsist;
Till each to raz'd oblivion yield his part
Of thee, thy record never can be miss'd.
That poor retention could not so much hold,
Nor need I tallies thy dear love to score;
Therefore to give them from me was I bold,
To trust those tables that receive thee more:
    To keep an adjunct to remember thee
    Were to import forgetfulness in me.

The World Is Too Much With Us

by William Wordsworth

The world is too much with us; late and soon,
Getting and spending, we lay waste our
      powers;—
Little we see in Nature that is ours;
We have given our hearts away, a sordid boon!
This Sea that bares her bosom to the moon;
The winds that will be howling at all hours,
And are up-gathered now like sleeping flowers;
For this, for everything, we are out of tune;
It moves us not. Great God! I'd rather be
A Pagan suckled in a creed outworn;
So might I, standing on this pleasant lea,
Have glimpses that would make me less forlorn;
Have sight of Proteus rising from the sea;
Or hear old Triton blow his wreathèd horn.

The Sand-Man

by Paul Laurence Dunbar

I know a man
  With face of tan,
But who is ever kind;
  Whom girls and boys
  Leaves games and toys
Each eventide to find.

  When day grows dim,
  They watch for him,
He comes to place his claim;
  He wears the crown
  Of Dreaming-town;
The sand-man is his name.

  When sparkling eyes
  Troop sleepywise
And busy lips grow dumb;

When little heads
Nod toward the beds,
We know the sand-man's come.

Peach Blossoms

by Hannah Flagg Gould

Come here! Come here! Cousin Mary, and see
What fair ripe peaches there are the tree—
On the very same bough that was given to me
By father, one day last spring.
When it look'd so beautiful, all in the blow,
And I wanted to pluck it, he told me, you know,
I might—but that waiting a few months would
  show
The fruit that patience might bring.

And, as I perceived by the sound of his voice,
And the look of his eye, it was clearly his choice
That it should not be touch'd, I have to now
  rejoice
  That I told him we'd let it remain.
For, had it been gather'd when full in the flower,
Its blossoms had wither'd, perhaps, in an hour,

And nothing on earth could have given the power
  That would make them flourish again!

But now, of a fruit so delicious and sweet
I've enough for myself, and my playmates a treat;
And they tell me, besides, that the kernels
  secrete
  What, if planted, will make other trees;
For the shell will come open to let down the
  root—
A sprout will spring up, whence the branches
  will shoot,
There'll be buds, leaves, and blossoms, and then
  comes the fruit—
  Such beautiful peaches as these!

And Nature, they say, like a mighty machine,
Has a wheel in a wheel, which, if ought comes
  between,
It ruins her work, as it might have been seen
  Had it not given patience this trial.

From this, I'll be careful to keep it in mind,

When the blossoms I love, that there lingers
behind

A better reward, that the trusting shall find

For a trifling self-denial!

Sonnet LXXXIV

by William Shakespeare

Who is it that says most? which can say more,
Than this rich praise,—that you alone, are you?
In whose confine immured is the store
Which should example where your equal grew?
Lean penury within that pen doth dwell
That to his subject lends not some small glory;
But he that writes of you, if he can tell
That you are you, so dignifies his story,
Let him but copy what in you is writ,
Not making worse what nature made so clear,
And such a counterpart shall fame his wit,
Making his style admired everywhere.
    You to your beauteous blessings add a curse,
    Being fond on praise, which makes your
        praises worse.

Jenny Wren

by Mother Goose

'Twas once upon a time,
when Jenny Wren was young,
So daintily she danced
and so prettily she sung,

Robin Redbreast lost his heart,
for he was a gallant bird;
So he doffed his hat to Jenny Wren,
requesting to be heard.

O, dearest Jenny Wren,
if you will but be mine,
You shall feed on cherry pie
and drink new currant wine,

I'll dress you like a goldfinch
or any peacock gay;

So, dearest Jen, if you'll be mine,
let us appoint the day.

Jenny blushed behind her fan
and thus declared her mind:
Since, dearest Bob, I love you well,
I take your offer kind;

Cherry pie is very nice
and so is currant wine,
But I must wear my plain brown gown
and never go too fine.

The Day Is Done

by Henry Wadsworth Longfellow

The day is done, and the darkness
    Falls from the wings of Night,
As a feather is wafted downward
    From an eagle in his flight.

I see the lights of the village
    Gleam through the rain and the mist,
And a feeling of sadness comes o'er me
    That my soul cannot resist:

A feeling of sadness and longing,
    That is not akin to pain,
And resembles sorrow only
    As the mist resembles the rain.

Come, read to me some poem,
    Some simple and heartfelt lay,

That shall soothe this restless feeling,
 And banish the thoughts of day.

Not from the grand old masters,
 Not from the bards sublime,
Whose distant footsteps echo
 Through the corridors of Time.

For, like strains of martial music,
 Their mighty thoughts suggest
Life's endless toil and endeavor;
 And to-night I long for rest.

Read from some humbler poet,
 Whose songs gushed from his heart,
As showers from the clouds of summer,
 Or tears from the eyelids start;

Who, through long days of labor,
 And nights devoid of ease,

Still heard in his soul the music
　　Of wonderful melodies.

Such songs have power to quiet
　　The restless pulse of care,
And come like the benediction
　　That follows after prayer.

Then read from the treasured volume
　　The poem of thy choice,
And lend to the rhyme of the poet
　　The beauty of thy voice.

And the night shall be filled with music,
　　And the cares, that infest the day,
Shall fold their tents like the Arabs,
　　And as silently steal away.

Cushy Cow Bonny

by Mother Goose

Cushy Cow bonny, let down your milk,

And I will give you a gown of silk,

A gown of silk and a silver tee,

If you'll let down your milk to me.

Morning Is the Place for Dew

by Emily Dickinson

Morning is the place for dew,
   Corn is made at noon,
After dinner light for flowers,
   Dukes for setting sun!

Infant Sorrow

by William Blake

My mother groaned! my father wept.
Into the dangerous world I leapt:
Helpless, naked, piping loud;
Like a fiend hid in a cloud.

Struggling in my father's hands:
Striving against my swaddling bands:
Bound and weary I thought best
To sulk upon my mother's breast.

To Mother

by Louisa May Alcott

I hope that soon, dear mother,
You and I may be
In the quiet room my fancy
Has so often made for thee,—

The pleasant, sunny chamber,
The cushioned easy-chair,
The book laid for your reading,
The vase of flowers fair;

The desk beside the window
Where the sun shines warm and bright:
And there in ease and quiet
The promised book you write;

While I sit close beside you,
Content at last to see

That you can rest, dear mother,
And I can cherish thee.

Richard and Robin

by Mother Goose

Richard and Robin were two pretty men;
They laid abed till the clock struck ten;
Robin starts up and looks at the sky,
Oh ho! brother Richard, the sun's very high,
Do you go before with the bottle and bag,
And I'll follow after on little Jack Nag.

The Eagle

by Alfred Lord Tennyson

He clasps the crag with crooked hands;
Close to the sun in lonely lands,
Ring'd with the azure world, he stands.

The wrinkled sea beneath him crawls;
He watches from his mountain walls,
And like a thunderbolt he falls.

Shoe the Colt

by Mother Goose

Shoe the colt,
Shoe the colt,
Shoe the wild mare;
Here a nail,
There a nail,
Colt must go bare.

Sonnet CXV

By William Shakespeare

Those lines that I before have writ do lie,
Even those that said I could not love you dearer:
Yet then my judgment knew no reason why
My most full flame should afterwards burn clearer.
But reckoning Time, whose million'd accidents
Creep in 'twixt vows, and change decrees of kings,
Tan sacred beauty, blunt the sharp'st intents,
Divert strong minds to the course of altering
    things;
Alas! why fearing of Time's tyranny,
Might I not then say, "Now I love you best,"
When I was certain o'er incertainty,
Crowning the present, doubting of the rest?
    Love is a babe, then might I not say so,
    To give full growth to that which still doth
        grow?

A Book

by Emily Dickinson

He ate and drank the precious words,
His spirit grew robust;
He knew no more that he was poor,
Nor that his frame was dust.
He danced along the dingy days,
And this bequest of wings
Was but a book. What liberty
A loosened spirit brings!

About Delia Berrigan

Delia Berrigan has written eleven books for children in addition to publishing and editing countless others. A literary agent for many years, when not representing authors or studying the latest in intellectual property and copyright law, she's chasing rainbows with her husband, daughters, and dogs in Kansas. Her father insists that the first poet in Ireland was also a Berrigan.

About Cider Mill Press Book Publishers

Good ideas ripen with time. From seed to harvest, Cider Mill Press brings fine reading, information, and entertainment together between the covers of its creatively crafted books. Our Cider Mill bears fruit twice a year, publishing a new crop of titles each spring and fall.

"Where Good Books Are Ready for Press"

501 Nelson Place
Nashville, Tennessee 37214

cidermillpress.com